Help and insight around dying

FONS DELNOOZ &

PATRICIA MARTINOT

This book has been translated from 'Hulp en inzicht rondom sterven'
(ISBN: 97890 202 03394) by Tanja Oldenziel.

ISBN – 10: 1508716617
ISBN-13: 978-1508716617

CONTENTS

Summary

Dying is... being born in another dimension. This statement raises many questions such as: what does the world look after death? What is the connection between that world and the one we are living in here on earth? How can we help people in the process of dying? Is contact possible after death?

The authors provide clear and transparent answers in this book. They explain what we can do and be of value for the dying person and for the soul after the body has died. The theory is constantly translated into 'how do you then apply it, what is possible?' It is a book for those that belief in life after death and want to deal with it in a meaningful way.

1 Death - what is death actually?

Dying, passing away, passing on, seem such clear words. They are not, because people attach completely different meanings to these words. One might regard death as the absolute ending. Conscience stops and the body perishes. Nothing remains. To others death represents the start of something new. A birth, we could call it, into a world that is different than our world. Being born in a world that we cannot perceive using our senses. "*Impossible,*" many say. "*There is no other world than the one we can perceive using our senses.*" "*There was never a person returning from death capable of telling us what this world would have to look like.*"

Surprising is that many people do rely that there is something after death, but they do not give it any thought. They do not investigate it. They also often have no idea how meaningful research in this area could be done. Their knowledge of the world awaiting them and their loved ones upon death is rudimentary. *"There is something after death, but what it is, I could not tell."*

It is actually amazing that many people expect that something continues yet do not put any effort into investigating the nature of that *something*! Firstly it is remarkable, because we will die ourselves and so do all our loved ones. We would want to know how we continue to live, right? Secondly, because there is so much knowledge about life after death. Knowledge that has been gathered in different ways, at different continents. Knowledge varying from having been written down thousands of years ago to knowledge being gained in our era. The major religions testify of a life after death. One tradition being more detailed than another. But they all agree: when the body dies, the soul continues to life.

Some religions support reincarnation. This concept is being confirmed by numerous personal experiences of people. There are people who can remember previous lives very accurately. Also small children, barely able to talk, sometimes talk about their previous lives in great details. At times they also speak in a language that is no longer spoken in such manner. Scientists have done research into the reliability of such information. Irrefutable it was concluded that some children could indeed describe details that were historically correct, of a time well before their birth. For example they know what the house and street looked like in their previous life. They know names and habits of people who were caring for them at the time.

Knowledge about death is also obtained through paranormal people, mediums. They possess the ability to connect with the soul of deceased people. Some can disconnect a part of their conscience from their body and travel to the world of the souls, the astral world. They describe extensively what the other world is looking like. There are people who are in close contact with souls in the other world, for example through direct communication. Sometimes, souls dictate entire books from the other world - word for word - for example about life on the other side.

To a large extent, knowledge about life after death arises through personal experiences related to it. When we experience strongly that there is another world in addition to the one, we perceive with our senses; it entails knowledge at the individual level that is reaching further than whichever book. Let us give two examples.

Sometimes people experience that the deceased person is paying them a visit. People in our practice volunteered, without us asking for it, and shared how they have had contact with a deceased person.

Esther (49): "When my husband had died, he occasionally came to visit me in the first weeks. I then saw him standing next to my bed. He smiled as he wanted to communicate that he was doing fine, and there was no need to worry."

The second example concerns near-death experiences. These occur when a person almost dies. The soul then disconnects from the body and reaches the other world. Often the soul is presented an overview lasting a few seconds or minutes of all her acts and thoughts in this life - and insight into the effect these have had on others. Sometimes there is contact with souls that have already moved on to the other world. Contact with angels is also often experienced. The near-death experiences last only a few minutes but lead in general to profound changes in the persons having experienced them.

2 The soul

The human being is a unity of three dimensions: the physical body, astral body and divine Spark. The term soul involves the latter two dimensions. Some use the term soul to refer to the astral body, other to refer to the Divine spark, and yet others to refer to the combination of the astral body and divine Spark. Everyone agrees that the soul is related to that part that continues to live when the body dies. Below, the terms astral body and divine Spark are first described before the soul is discussed.

The astral body

The astral body continues to live when the physical body dies. Both the astral and physical body are constructed of energy but the energy of the physical body is slower resulting in a relatively solid appearance. The astral body possesses a higher vibrational level, which our ordinary senses are not attuned to. Some people are capable of (partly) perceiving the astral body. For example, they can feel it with their hands, or see the energy field around a person. These observations are not made using the physical senses but with ethereal senses that form part of the astral body.

Several properties of the astral body are similar to the earthly body: thinking, remembering and recalling, feeling and communicating. The astral body can also relocate. During the life on earth, it is closely cooperating with the physical body. Thinking and feeling are occurring in tight collaboration between the astral and the physical body. Let's look at the following example.

Mrs Peterson is being operated, and she has been fully anaesthetised. After the operation, she tells, "... I have seen and been part of everything. I was floating above my body, just below the ceiling. I have seen every detail from start to finish. I experienced how they treated me. I have felt they treated me without respect. I could not understand this. I felt utterly powerless. I could not interfere as my body was anaesthetised. Now, four days after the operation, I am still completely upset they treated me in such a manner. They executed a procedure we had not agreed upon. They took something away!"

Mrs Peterson is pressing charges. The details she is sharing match what has actually taken place in the surgical theatre. Mrs Peterson had perceived through her astral body. It allowed her to see, hear, read others, feel, reason and draw conclusions. She was capable of doing what she usually would use her physical body for. The only thing she could not do was informing the world (of human beings) *because her body was made inoperative by the anaesthetics.*

The divine Spark

The divine Spark is an extraordinary part of the human being. It is the spark of divine Light. It is pure conscience. It is pure life energy. It forms the core of each human being, his centre. This divine Spark is absolute love. She radiates her love and conscience to the person. When we focus inward and feel deep, pure love within ourselves, we are aware of this divine Spark.

Some people are in full direct contact with their divine Spark. In the Christian tradition, this is referred to as a mystic experience. In the East, it is called enlightenment. People who experience this describe the world as exceptionally beautiful and loving. Everything is one; they say. There is total, all-encompassing love. There is endless conscience, endless knowledge, and endless space.

The above described the beauty corresponding to when we are one with our divine Spark. The human being also possesses a different side: not being in contact with the divine Spark. As a result, one feels dark, depressed, isolated, and meaningless. Nothing seems useful. There is no love. It can lead to despondency, giving up altogether. It can also turn into hatred and violence.

The human being is thus capable of having direct intense contact with his divine Spark, or being entirely disconnected. Most people will be somewhere in the middle. Every person is on a path to being one with his divine Spark. The road toward it is unique, because the human being possesses free will and is living within the duality of light and dark. Each second, we make (unconscious) choices in our behaviour that either bring us closer to our divine Spark or in the opposite direction. This concept applies to any aspect in life, for example, thoughts, what we look at, listen to, eat, and drink. Again and again, it holds that one choice is purer and thus bringing closer to the divine Spark, and the other choice darker and thus leading a person away from his divine Spark.

People living their lives from the light are more directly linked to their divine Spark. They feel the love in their heart, which is the expression of the divine Spark in them. They are also more aware of the signals that the divine Spark is emanating. They act more according to the higher truth in their heart. *Not my will, but yours be done* as it says in the Bible.

The soul

As mentioned earlier, the human being possesses three dimensions: the physical body, the astral body and the divine Spark. When a person dies, the physical body perishes. We take off a coat we no longer need. What remains are the astral body and divine Spark. Now what is then referred to as the soul? In the Christian tradition, the soul refers to what remains alive after the body dies. Thus, the soul is the astral body and divine Spark combined. Some people are aware that something like the divine Spark exists, other do not see or acknowledge it.

In the Eastern tradition, the soul relates directly to the divine Spark. The astral body is being seen as a body that covers the soul such that is can live in the astral world. It is just a body, similar to the physical body being an adaptation to allow for life in the earthly world comparable to an astronaut. To be able to operate in space, he needs to adapt his body: he is wearing a space suit that regulates the pressure and breathing. Without it, he would not be able to function. Each environment requires an adaption of the body. Similarly, the divine Spark needs different bodies to work in the astral and earthly world. In the Eastern, and in particular the Vedic tradition, the term atman or jiva-atman is often used for the divine Spark. The soul is thus atman or divine Spark.

The above might logically lead to miscommunication in written and spoken word. Different definitions are given to the word soul, which is directly related to the level of insight the author is capable of regarding the being of humans. To one, the divine Spark is a reality; to someone else it is an unknown concept.

In this book, the term divine Spark will be used for the divine Self that is equally present in each human being. The term soul we use for that part that remains alive when the physical body has died: the astral body and within it the magnificent radiating Spark of Light: the divine Spark. When the body dies, the soul continues living in another space. How does this world look? How does this world differ from our world and how is it similar? The next chapter will tackle these questions.

3 The astral world: the world of souls without a body

To some extent, the life of the soul in the astral world is similar to the life of a human being on earth. The first similarity is that the soul is *living* in the astral world! The soul is aware who she is, subjectively. She has a clear idea of her environment, after having gotten used to her new surroundings after death. She can be happy and joyful, but also intensely sad and angry. She can be in contact with other souls. She has excellent abilities to communicate. Empathy is at times much more direct and intense than on earth: other souls can be read very quickly.

Duality, free will and the law of karma: the development of the human being on earth and the soul in the astral world

Souls can be jubilant, but also unhappy. Differently said: they are living within duality, just like we do on earth. Duality means that everything consists of opposites. The duality forms one of the main pillars beneath the development of the human being and his soul. Because the entire world is being experienced as opposites, we can experience the characteristics of these poles. We can be cold, or warm. Experience love or loneliness. We can do good, but also evil.

The second pillar of the development of the human being and his soul is free will. The human being has access to free will in order to choose within the duality, which life is continuously offering. Do I opt for 'good' or 'no-good'? This option is available, every moment of the day, to every person. Doing nothing is also a choice - sometimes it is supporting the 'good' and sometimes it is a choice that is strengthening the 'no-good' in this world.

The human being is thus living in a dual world, within which he is free to choose. How does this environment lead to awareness? The answer is a third nature law that exists. What we sow is what we reap, teaches the Bible. What we do, comes back manifold to us, in the short or long run. Do we do 'good'; the good will return to us manifold, now or later. The same applies to the no-good. It is an entirely neutral mirror. Not the hand of an evil revengeful God, but a law that allows us to learn from our acts. In the Eastern philosophy this is called the law of karma, where karma means act. The goal? The goal is to become one, in free will, with our divine Spark. It is the essence both here on earth as well as in the astral world. Unification with our divine Spark is being experienced as total unity with all that is and thus as limitless love.

The fundamental laws - duality, free will and the law of karma - function in both worlds in exactly the same manner because both worlds serve the same purpose. They enable a development leading to the coinciding of the personal self with the divine Self (the divine Spark). In Christian terms, it is referred to as the birth of Christ conscience in the human being. The development of the human being consists of three pillars:

Duality: we live in a dual environment, where light versus dark form the most important opposites (poles).

Free will: a dual environment requires that we always take a stand. What do we choose? Each thought, word and act are an expression of a choice, which lies somewhere between the poles of light and dark. We are hundred per cent free in our choice - always!

Law of karma: we are hundred per cent responsible for our choices. What we do comes back to us amplified, in long or short run.

Differences between the astral and earthly world

The most significant difference between the earthly and astral world is the degree of compaction. The vibrational level of our world is much lower than the energy of the astral world. The material world is so much more compact than the astral world that it requires changing it through physical effort. Whatever we do, asks for time and effort. Do we want our house to be a different colour? We either have to paint it ourselves or pay a painter using money we have first earned. In the astral world, the process is of a different nature; the environment is psycho-plastic. In the astral world our environment forms (plastic) under the influence of our feelings and thoughts (psycho). When we have sombre feelings, a sombre grey world instantly arises around us. Are we euphoric, then the surroundings immediately change and become a reflection of our feeling of happiness. As you feel inside, such is the world around you.

How different it is here on earth. Somebody can be very unhappy, but the sun is still shining, the flowers growing, the birds chirping and the girl next door smiling to her mum. Still the psycho-plastic principle does operate here on earth, be it less direct. Through our thoughts here on earth we also form an environment. For example, when we are convinced that a tough task is a fantastic challenge that we will master, then most likely we will. Countless therapies use this principle. All major spiritual traditions and many masters and wise people, point the human being, again and again, in the direction of the power of his thoughts. Use this power to your benefit, is the advice. The principle thus functions here on earth as well, but not as direct as in the astral world.

Because the astral environment forms after our inner being, we are continuously in an environment of like-spirited souls in the astral world. When we feel much love inside, we are in a very light environment with extremely loving souls. When we experience the darkness in us, the surroundings are also dark. The souls around us are neither happy nor radiant. Also, very dark worlds exist of souls that live in hatred and fear. The collection of these intensely dark worlds is called the low-astral world. The world of light, on the other hand, is called the high-astral world. To say that there are only two dimensions: light and dark, is a simplification of reality. There is a continuum ranging from the most extreme dark to the most radiant light. The division in the two worlds (high and low astral) fits with the Christian tradition, which refers to heaven and hell. Heaven is then the world in which we are connected inside with love and thus, following the law of that world, are in an environment of light. Hell is the environment in which love is not known and where fears and hatred rule. When we look at it this way, we see that heaven is not a reward from God and hell not a punishment from God. It is nothing else, but the magnification of what we experience inside us. An entirely neutral mirror. It is how the cosmos has been organised, aiming to help us become aware of our choices. Such that we eventually, in free will, make those decisions that bring us home, to our divine Spark.

Souls in the astral world can also move. They do not have to buy train tickets, nor gasoline. They are exactly there, where their thoughts are focusing. It occurs extremely quickly. Within a fraction of a second, they can cross distances of thousands of kilometres. It might seem strange and fast, but sunlight travels at 300.000 kilometres per second, where sunlight is part of the visible spectrum. It is more compact than our thoughts. The speed of thoughts is many times faster than that of light. Therefore, in the astral world, distance is a relative concept.

Summarising, we can state that a large difference between the earthly and the astral world lies in the psycho-plastic character of the astral world. The astral world is, therefore, organised in fields of like-sorted emotional, mental and spiritual levels. The soul is in the environment at which he is focusing. This insight is paramount in providing help to those dying and to souls that have already moved on to the astral world. We explain this in more detail in the next chapter.

4 Life on earth determines life in the astral world

Many people like to know what their financial future will look like once they retire. They are being advised to investigate what they already have invested into their pension plan and what they are intending to invest in the coming years. Whoever wants to know what life after death (pension) will look like, has to investigate his thoughts and feelings (his investments) now. There are two research questions to focus on:

- *Are my thoughts, words, feelings and deeds focused on the light, or more on the dark? To what extent are they more light or more dark?*

- *How stable am I in this space?*

At this moment, imagine positive thoughts, feelings, words, and deeds... Around us, an environment of like-minded people arises. Similarly positive, and supportive as we are ourselves. What effect does it have? Most likely, it is lifting us up, and we are becoming even more positively minded. What would the opposite be? Our thoughts, feelings, words, and deeds are more geared toward the negative. An environment develops around us with people radiating the same as we do. How does that feel? We probably feel even more miserable.

In both scenarios, the outer world has formed after the inner world. It is how the astral world operates due to its psycho-plastic nature. The happy and caring human being has not become this way overnight. It is the character of that human being. When a human being dies, he does not take along his possessions. Also, his looks stay on earth. What he does take along is what we call here on earth his character. This character is the mother of his thoughts and feelings. This happy and caring person is taking a pleasant and caring character to the astral world. His thoughts and feelings in the astral world will be happy and caring. His environment will have a similar character. The more loving a person is on earth, the more beautiful the world will be in which he will live after his death. Isn't that a fantastic idea? The more beautiful we are on earth, the more beautiful the world will be when we die. When we want a pleasant place in the astral world, it requires of us that we live a loving life with high moral standards.

The above knowledge is part of the writings of the large religious traditions. Each aims to help the human being in leading a righteous life in the sense of a morally just and caring life. Each major tradition might focus on different aspects but in essence all point out the same.

When we want to help ourselves in achieving dying in a proper way and leading a good life after death, we can work on it now: by living in a righteous, morally just and caring manner. It is easier said than done; the life of almost everyone shows that it does not come quickly. Our work as therapists is essentially about this aspect. How can we be in contact with ourselves such that we are love, pure and just? It is first and foremost dependent on the contact we have with our heart.

The heart possesses two dimensions. The one dimensions is within duality, and at this level, a person can feel the love, but also terrible pain. The pain is the result of experiencing a lack of love and all possible reactions to it: withdrawal, hatred, anger, loneliness, suffering, wanting to hurt others, giving up, depression, ... This part of the heart we refer to as the *small heart*. The other dimension, we refer to as the *big heart*.

The *big heart* in its most pure conscience is divine Love. It is always present and completely unconditional. It is the divine Spark. She always radiates love toward ourselves, toward the person we are in this life on earth. She invites us to come to her, become one with her. The closer we get to our Source of Light, the more radiating we become. We become caring - because that is the essential characteristic of the divine Spark. We become full of power and self-conscientious, not in the sense of an ego that is out of proportion, but we know what is right and what not. We know this well because love - and only love - has the ultimate discernment over what is just. We live a morally pure life and are following high moral standards because we neither can nor want to do differently.

This magnificent big heart is present in every human being. In each human being is it equally radiant and inviting. But not every human being can connect with it and be led by it due to the pain body. The pain body is the still active collection of all the pains we have experienced. The pain body continuously gives instructions to the psyche how we have to act, especially in relation to love. For example, it instructs us to close our heart and takes adequate measure to do so. The presence of the pain body deprives us of our sight of our magnificent big heart. Often people identify with their pain body, which results in them entirely agreeing with all the reactions initiated in that part within them. It is expressed in negative thoughts and words, and at times also harmful deeds. These thoughts, words and deeds are speaking to and activating the pain body of others. The pain body thus receives confirmation and develops in the wrong direction: depriving us even more of who we are in essence: our big heart. When we want to progress as humankind and as individual beings, it requires distancing from our pain body and experiencing we are something else than that pain body. It is also a prerequisite for a life full of love here on earth, and a loving environment after the physical body has died. Practically, it means that it is good to let go of negative thoughts and emotions. It also asks that we learn to handle pain in a healthy and above all efficient manner. This process will be discussed in the next chapter as well as in detail in a downloadable hand out *Dealing with Emotions*.

Conclusion

The more loving, righteous and morally pure our lives have been here on earth; the more loving, righteous and morally pure a world awaits us after our death. It is the fundamental law. To live lovingly requires that we can process our pain efficiently. Otherwise, the pain fixated in our pain body could deprive us of our sight of who we essentially are: a Being of Love.

5 Dealing with feelings related to dying

The death of someone close always has an impact on us. The intensity depends on the relationship we had with the person that passed on. It is also dependent on how we are dealing with our feelings. Where one person might be capable of feeling at a deeper level, another has less contact with his feelings. Dealing with a loss is a complex process, in which many aspects play a role. In this chapter, tools are given to provide help in dealing with the loss.

It is hurtful when a person dies, with whom we felt a deep connection. Sometimes it hurts considerably. At times so much that it deprives us of our breath. We have the feeling we cannot handle it. The body then intervenes; part of the pain is being blocked. It is being set aside for later. Often it is called denial. Denial is chosen, because it is the only method to survive, to keep going. However, the day will come, when we cannot deny any longer. Suddenly, or gradually, the pain is breaking through. Layer for layer we are opening for what we have tucked away earlier. It can take weeks, months or even years before we get in contact with that denied pain. It may take many years before we dare to allow feeling all aspects of it. Year after year we process deeper, and space arises to dare feel what we denied earlier. Moreover, then life moves on; very carefully we stand up again. It will never be the same. Processing the loss of someone we truly love is a process of trial and error, of again and again being confronted with the pain and loss in all its aspects.

Also, the soul that has moved on is going through a similar process. The process of letting go of what was and facing a new environment. We can no longer be in contact with our loved one the way we used to. Talking together, holding hands, it is no longer possible. Contact at an essential level is still possible. We can still feel the deceased one. We can even talk to him. The contact will continue to fill our hearts - because the deceased one is very much alive. Thus, we can open our heart to this lively deceased person. Feeling love, feeling it deeply. Then we can experience that the living deceased person is still very close. After a person has died, we may and can be in contact with the soul of the deceased one. This connection is real, simply because the deceased one is still very much active, be it in a different dimension. Spiritual contact might provide comfort. Pain remains because the pain is unavoidable in most situations of loss. It is most important that we feel, feel and keep on feeling. When we do not avoid the pain, but dare to approach it, it forms the opening to healing of the pain.

Feeling pain means truly connecting with the pain, by experiencing the rawness and avoiding nothing. When we truly feel the pain, processing of it takes place. Often we flee from the pain. The breathing becomes quick and rises into the chest. Sometimes the breathing is then very shallow, almost limited to the collarbones. We in- and exhale quickly. We might feel to some extent but are fleeing to avoid the pain. There is little to no digestion of the pain. We do suffer but do not process the pain. It is a shame of the suffering, if not used for a good cause. When the breathing lowers into the abdomen, the organs can process the energy of the emotions. Processing of the emotions works best when the breathing reaches all the way to the lower abdomen. It is also important that the exhalation be long because it represents letting go. When the exhalation is twice as long as the inhalation, the system can let go to a deeper level and more effectively than when in- and exhalation are equally long. The length of the breathing also plays a role: three seconds in and six seconds out is a nice balance. Whoever breathes into their abdomen and feels, is digesting (emotions) effectively.

'Properly feeling' does deserve some explanation. It means that we focus all our attention at what we feel. It can be emotional pain, but also something being blocked in our body, for example, tension near the heart. We process by placing our attention continuously at the strongest feeling and remaining there until the feeling subsides. Then another feeling might arise, or tightness at another part of the body, which we can treat in the same manner. It is how we peel off layer by layer. There will be a day we do not feel pain anymore, but calmness and softness. The step-by-step technique to process emotions follows below. A more detailed digital description is found online: *Dealing with Emotions*.

Exercise - Processing emotions

1. Feel your belly. It is where you place your attention.

2. Be aware of your breathing rhythm and count.

3. Try to breathe 3 seconds in and 6 seconds out. Stick to this rhythm during the entire exercise, especially when you are experiencing intense emotions or feeling physical pain. At the inhalation, the abdomen moves outward, at the exhalation the abdomen moves inward. Inhale through the nose and exhale through the mouth.

4. Feel. Do you feel emotions or physical tension? Both are equally meaningful. Focus entirely at what feels most intense. Continue breathing in your abdomen, long exhalations, even when you feel you are (getting) emotional. Without the long exhalation, this exercise does not work.

5. Do thoughts and images arise? Do not give them any attention, but focus on what feels strongest.

6. When this feeling becomes less intense, it has been processed as deeply as is possible right now. It may happen in a few seconds, but longer as well. Observe if another feeling is asking for your

attention. Repeat steps 4 and 5 for this new feeling.

7. Continue, repeating, as long as is feeling good to you. When you have spent ten to twenty minutes, and intense emotions continue to arise, it is advisable to stop and pick it up at another time.

8. End the exercise always with a strong image or thought that gives you a pleasant, positive, powerful feeling.

Daring to feel deeply and breathing correctly at the same time is essential for a healthy and efficient dealing with loss. There is also another method. It is related to the big heart, the divine Spark present in everyone. When we succeed to be in contact with our divine Spark, we can live life based on this contact. Then we can deal with the pain knowing the reality of that deep, inner feeling of being carried - even when the world around us is collapsing. There is still pain, deep pain as well, but it feels far less raw. An inner knowing is present that all is well, despite the pain. It facilitates bearing the pain at the personal level more easily and, as a result, processing it. Because if we can handle the pain, we do not have to walk away from it. If we can remain with the pain, the process of digestion is taking place.

How can we connect with our divine Spark? Alternatively, how can this connection be deepened and strengthened? In essence, it is about whether we truly dare to allow love in our being. When we dare to experience love, we are closer to our inner Source of light and love. Opening the heart to love is thus a powerful method to be in contact with the inner Source. It is a very direct option.

Deep pain makes it at times hard to be in contact with the inner Source of love, our inner divine Spark. It is because we do not want to feel in this area of the heart. The pain is as a grey mist covering our sight of the divine Spark. When facing the pain, the mist dissolves, and we can be in contact with our divine Spark.

When we properly are in touch with the divine Spark, it is possible to transcend much pain. We can connect with the divine Spark and simultaneously, as a person, suffer. We then move our conscience from suffering to the divine Spark. It aids us in letting go of the pain, and it assists us in feeling carried while we suffer. Below exercise focuses on connecting with the divine Spark.

Exercise - Opening the heart using rose quartz

1. Open the heart to rose quartz. If needed use gratitude to open the heart.

2. Imagine that the rose quartz is emitting pink light.

3. Allow this light to enter at the middle of your breastbone all the way to the backbone.

4. Place your attention at this spot at the inside of your backbone.

5. Place the rose quartz at this position.

6. Let the pink light shine in all directions within your heart. Relax. Enjoy the warm feeling that the rose quartz generates in your heart.

7. Let the light of the rose quartz radiate forward and backward through the skin. Remain with your attention in the rose quartz, at your backbone.

8. Feel the entire area where the rose quartz radiates as one.

9. Make an inner decision that this light continues to shine until you leave this body.

10. Open your eyes. Feel the pink light.

11. Look around you. Feel the pink light.

12. Intend that this pink light keeps flowing your entire life, until you leave this life.

Children

Also, children can be confronted with the loss of someone important to them: a sibling, a parent, or others. We have heard many stories of our clients about losing someone in their childhood and how they dealt with it.

I was eight years. My sister was already ill for some days. Suddenly the ambulance arrived. I was being ushered into another room. My sister was being brought to the hospital. A few days later she was dead. I have not seen her anymore. I did not have a chance to say goodbye. I was not allowed to be at the funeral. At home, we did not talk about what had happened. All of a sudden she was not there anymore. Never did we talk about her: as if she has never been.

When I was six, my father died. I did not go to the funeral. We have never spoken about it. Only much later, when I was in my twenties, I dared to talk about it with my mum.

Parents try to protect their children from the pain. It is a natural, instinctive habit. When the parent sets the example that the death is something to not talk about, a child senses this faultlessly. Often before the parents express it, the children pick it up and act accordingly. However, children cannot be protected from experiencing the loss through death because it is there - all day long. When a sister has died, pretending she does not exist does not solve it because the sister was part of the family, part of everyday life.

Children are allowed to process (pain) in their way. In order to achieve this, it is required that pain be allowed to be. Completely, visibly, tangibly. It is important that the child be allowed to ask all questions. The child is asking the questions for a reason. It is on his mind; it makes him wonder. He wants to have an answer. The child deserves honest answers. The questions are part of the process within the child. Children go through the process at their pace, in their unique way. They are allowed to differ in this. It is good to recognise this. Give each child its possibilities to handle the pain. Some children might require going through a long process that asks for attention and time.

Young children are closer to the astral world than adults. It allows them to make contact easier with the deceased ones. It is important to recognise this and to take children seriously. When a small child informs you that the grandpa has been visiting him, you can assume that this took place, even when grandpa died a month earlier.

When a family member dies, the world collapses. Also to the child. Therefore, it is important that the child feels supported by the parent that it continues to feel safe. It is the parent's task to provide this safety. The parent does not provide this security through a total denial of the situation to the child and neither by not communicating his feelings to the child. Explain that it is part of the process, that it is normal. That it may take a while but that things will be better at a later stage. It is like in winter when it is freezing; after a while, it warms up again, and you can nicely play outside again. However, when the sorrow is overwhelming for a parent, it is important to restrict expressing all of it toward the child.

To a child, it is welcoming when it can do something for a deceased family member. In chapter seven, it will be discussed how we can *place a (deceased) person in the light*. We refer to imagining (inside our big heart) that the astral body of the deceased person entirely radiates light from his own divine Spark. Children can also do this. It often comes easier to them than to adults, because these types of acts take place at the astral level. It has not been that long ago that a child lived there. They are much closer to it than adults.

It is also pleasant for children when a 'shrine' is created at home for the deceased one. You can create it, as you like. Important is that it is a pleasant place, with good memories. You can for example include a few beautiful pictures, a drawing, fresh flowers, a burning candle, an incense holder, a crystal, a small icon or a model that represents the higher world of angels, Buddha, Jesus, Maria or whoever is preferred or fitting. The shrine provides a pleasant place to honour the deceased person every day. It offers an opportunity to send love and light, as a family, and to ask God, the angels, Jesus, or whomever we feel connected to, to take care of the deceased one. Doing so, keeps the deceased person in our midst in a beautiful way. Space naturally arises in which we can be together in our sorrow and can help each other by listening to each other and giving sincere attention. It is a powerful engine for the necessary process of dealing with the loss, also for children.

There are several remedies available that can be used to help children develop themselves with regard to the dying of a loved one. As therapists, we have very positive experiences with them. Especially the very young ones respond exceptionally well when these remedies are offered. We think of flower remedies, crystal elixirs, homeopathy, essential oils and Aura-Soma products. Within the standard care system, the use of these remedies is not widely known. Outside of it, they are loved, especially because they are so well suited for self-help (except for homeopathy) and are effective. Where standard medical remedies mainly anesthetise and suppress, the energetic level remedies show to the child the road ahead. Because the human being is a unity of his physical body, his energetic body and his divine Spark, these remedies work profoundly, in all his layers. In addition, these remedies are cheap and freely available. In our experience, children are very well capable of choosing these remedies themselves. Let's look at an example.

Joyce is six years old. Her best friend Lily passed away the previous week. Karin, her mum, has taken her to a shop selling flower remedies. When they are standing in front of the shelves with remedies, Karin talks briefly about the deceased friend bringing the attention of Joyce to the theme. Then Karin asks: "Which bottle could help you best now that Lily has died?" Joyce is looking at the bottles. Resolutely she picks a bottle. Her choice is accurate, clear.

6 When the soul releases the body: the process of dying

Here, we describe what happens during the process of dying. It provides insight into how we can be present, and be of help during this process including the added value to the moving on soul.

What happens when we die

When we are dying, body functions are slowing down, and activity levels are decreasing. It can happen rapidly, for example in a fatal heart attack or car accident. It can also be a process that stretches over a longer period. As mentioned earlier, the human being is an entirety of the physical body, the astral body and the divine Spark. The three units intertwine with the life of a human being. In the process of dying one of the parts, the physical body, is being repelled.

The process of dying can be a peaceful process. It can also be experienced as painful, confusing, and frightening.

When death is not sudden but gradual, the functioning of the senses is continuously decreasing. First, we still perceive but we can place less and less meaning in what we observe. We hear sounds, see shapes, but cannot interpret them anymore. The ability to communicate through the body decreases and eventually stops. The mouth dries up further and further. Urine and defecation run without us having control over both any longer. Our mind may get more confused Often relative clarity and confusion alternate. The collaboration between the ethereal bodies and the physical body is being deconstructed. The soul is retreating from the body. Then comes the moment that the last breath is being exhaled. To the Western medical science we are then dead. A process is still on-going in which the ethereal body continues to further disconnect from the physical body. This process can take up to three days. It explains why in several traditions it is being advised to hold a wake during the three days following the clinical death. Later in the book this is explained in more detail.

Astral clarity

When a person closer to death is becoming more confused or physically entirely incapable of communicating any longer, the astral body is taking charge of the communication. The astral body is fully capable of communicating with the people that are present around the dying person. It is hearing what they are saying, and accurately feeling the intentions of their presence. However, the communication is usually one-sided. The astral body sees, hears and feels, but it cannot communicate any of it to the people present because the these people are set to communicate through their physical body. Only the very (energy) sensitive and clairvoyant people are capable of perceiving the signals sent by the astral body of a dying person.

People who are nearly dead perceive us, while we are often not aware of it. It also applies to people who are in a coma or completely anesthetised. When we treat them with little respect and love, it is hurtful to them.

7 To help in the process of dying and being born

How can we approach the dying person such that he benefits from it most? That is the theme of this chapter. It is a complex topic. To help during the process of dying is so much more than just assisting the person to leave the body with the least amount of pain. It is, above all, also helping to be born again, in the best possible way, into a new world. Both are inextricably connected.

We ended the previous chapter with guidelines how we could deal with the dying person who is no longer capable of perceiving through his physical body. The soul of the dying person still perceives us clearly: she is hearing, seeing, feeling and knowing everything through her astral body. Approach her thus with the deepest respect. Everything we say is heard!

The world into which the soul will be born is psycho-plastic in nature. She forms after the feelings and thoughts of the soul. The more balanced the soul is during the process of dying; the more stable the world will be in which she initially arrives. How can we help in this? Again we refer to the above directions. The dimension supporting these guidelines is love. Love is the most important factor in the process of moving on, as we will call the entirety of dying and being born again in the remainder of the book.

The world to which the soul is moving is the astral world, which has been mentioned earlier in the book. One part of the astral world possesses more love, the high astral world, the other less love, the low astral world. These extreme poles spanning from total light to complete darkness are huge worlds apart. Where do we allow the dying person to be born? When we want to help the dying person, we long with all our being and soul that he will be born in the world of light and not just that, but as high into the light as possible given his development. When we lovingly approach the dying person, space arises in which many dying people naturally turn toward the light, as deep as they want and are capable. This light is the birth channel to the higher worlds in the astral world. Our love is the bridge supporting the dying person to die in love and thus to be born in the world of light. The above illustrates how beautiful and magnificent the tasks is of helping a person in the process of dying.

Whoever takes on this task, may thus be a platform of love. He may open to the most beautiful in himself and express this in his behaviour, words, attitude, and care for the dying person. It is a unique mission. Indeed, because the person most connected to the dying person is often also the one suffering most of the other dying. These two elements form a field of tension, which not everyone can unite. Therefore, we offer some tools. We do very well realise that it is dependent on the depth of development and the nature of the relationship at which level it is possible to blend the two aspects.

When a loved one is dying, and we have taken up the role to help him move on, a unique space arises. A space that we possibly have never experienced. In the first place, there is time. With the death approaching, everything that once seemed so important disappears. We do not go to work. We are probably helped in our care for, and maybe also by, our children. There are time and space to be with the dying person. Unique! What an extraordinary chance. It is an opportunity to cherish. Now everything is possible, especially because death shows us the relativity of our daily tasks and rhythms. To a certain extent it is also 'now or never'.

It is important to provide a pleasant atmosphere around the dying person. Privacy is paramount, both for the dying as well as the visitors. It is pleasant if an atmosphere can be created that feels their own and, if an energy can be built allowing for love and compassion. It has a positive effect if the space is well cared for and continues to be kept up well.

It merely creates a better environment and invites the higher in the human being; the higher that is so important in the process of dying. The room can be decorated with beautiful flowers, and with pleasant soft colours. Candlelight is important, because it adds to the energy in the room. Light always represents the higher aspect and the pure. We burn candles to call forth both. Fire is burning, and burning is a form of change. The dying, moving on, is a large transformation that may occur in the power of light from the fire.

Within the care of time and a well cared for environment, the possibility presents itself to be soft and tender and to let the heart entirely speak of love. Now, there are moments in which we can also show our love toward the other. Know that each word will be accepted in great gratitude. Know that behind each piece of body language, each word, each gesture of love or tenderness of the dying person there is a whole world of love, now that the body's communication capacity is limited. This love is of an enormous power. It can also, in some aspects, make us feel exceptionally good. We feel powerful and strong. We communicate clearly and purely what we could not express in this way before. Limitations disappear. We feel love. We feel connected with the dying person. When we are keeping a wake for a long time, serene silence can develop inside us, which has a meditative character. We feel carried by the light. We then do not feel alone. It is very special, because a loved one is leaving this world. We will not be able to connect with him in the ways we used to. Still, the love can transcend all this. These are the wings we can give our loved one on his journey.

At the same time, there can be pain, at times an intense pain. Old wounds are opened yielding sharp pain. Hatred may become poignant. The pain body will try and ask for attention in any possible manner, and will try to show itself. How can we deal with this? We know that the dark feelings may direct the dying person toward the dark worlds in the astral world. We also know that the process of moving on thus will be delayed. The same applies to feelings such as *I need you; do not leave me alone; I cannot live without you!* It explains why it is so important to achieve peace with the dying person before the dying process sets in. This process of palliative care starts thus well before the actual death begins. It shows how crucial it is to express what we feel and think. Finding a balance again, together, once it has been distorted. Here we can think, for example, of the relation of a child to a parent. Tensions and desires are at times not communicated for decades. The process of dying teaches us to solve in the now what is important to sort out. Moreover, what to think of a sudden, unexpected death? This possibility - that we will all get to face - emphasises even more the role of good communication that allows solving pain, such that we can again treat each other with respect and love.

How true these words may be, the situation for many people is not this ideal. Would it then be necessary to express everything during the process of dying? The following considerations may play a role in answering this question: The most important aim of palliative care is to create peace in the heart of a person moving on. Perhaps expressing some of the issues might be of help. May this then be the case. Maybe there is not much value for the dying person in our words, let alone our (corresponding) charges. Is it possible to let go of these charges for now? Is it possible to connect with another space in ourselves? We transcend our pain body and get into a larger space in our heart. Whether it is possible, will depend on many individual factors. For example, how powerful is the charge in the pain body; how identified are we with this load? Are we used to let go of the pain body and step into a bigger space, or is this potentially an option we are not familiar with and have little to no relevant skills?

Imagine, we regard it as not possible or not desirable to transcend our pain body, what happens then when we express our pain toward the person dying? Does it open the road in ourselves to real love? Then that could logically be of meaning. When it opens us to even more anger and sorrow, which we have no clue how to handle, does it help at that moment? Know that it is also possible at a later stage, also long after the person has died, to communicate with the loved one that has moved on. Maybe that is a better timing. Later in the book, we explain how to contact the soul that has moved on.

Spirituality

Spirituality is a term that people define differently. In this book, spirituality is about the contact of the human being with God: the deeper and more substantial our connection with God, the more spiritual we are. Spirituality is about knowing that the soul continues to live when the body dies, and that there is life after death. Spiritual knowledge also teaches us about life after death. She also explains how life in the astral world is connected to how we live on earth. Spirituality is getting to know ourselves.

Spirituality is of enormous importance for the dying and the person helping. For the carer, it provides comfort and a clear frame for the support. To the dying person it is a travel guide to his new environment. Deep-rooted spirituality transcends the fear of suffering and the fear for the future both for the dying person and the one providing care. It also gives meaning and significance to the process of moving on.

Imagine a woman giving birth to her first child while her birth channel is inexperienced, and she is scared for the pain that might be and the powers that might arise in her. Whom does she prefer to have around her? Someone who is familiar with the whole process and radiating strength and calm or someone who is impatient and tense about what is to happen? When a child is receiving his first inoculation, whom does it feel carried by: a calm mum with an open heart present with her child or a mum fearful of the reaction of the child?

To the dying person, it is a blessing if the carer dares to surrender to God. When he dares to trust that what is happening, has to happen. When he dares to relax and let go. Spirituality makes this possible. Deep spirituality, knowledge about the process of dying and being born, allow that we accept what is happening. It supports the person in his dying. If we, as a helper, trust that the right thing happens and that it is what has to happen now, then we carry the dying person, maybe even more than in any other way. Know that the dying person perceives through his astral body. It is about the contact we have with ourselves, not about empty, meaningless words. This message of surrendering to God can also be communicated entirely without words. It can also be worded while the dying is sleeping or in a coma. The message will be received.

Communicating about life after death

Not everybody finds it easy to talk about death. Some people avoid the subject until their last exhalation. It shows again how important it is to make dying part of living. It is something that is part of life, just like birth and birthdays. When we do not talk about death and spirituality while alive, how can we then die? Where do we begin? The skill gap is enormous. We can regard this as spiritual illiteracy. It is not meant as a nasty remark, but as ascertaining a fact. To be able to survive in society, we need to be able to read and write. To be able to die, it is essential to have a profound insight into what dying is, what we can expect and how we can positively impact it.

It is a fact that very few people bother to dive into the topic of dying during their lives. Nonetheless, death is also approaching for their loved ones and themselves. How can we help these people when they die? What is the best way to help them along, such that they reach the best spot? Starting point is the psycho-plastic character of the other world. What we want is that the other moves on in peace and love, such that he can be born in the world of peace and love. When a carer is capable of creating this space in himself, he creates a framework in which the dying person can move along. In general, it is important to stay close to the thoughts of a dying person. Otherwise, he does not feel heard or seen and might tend to be angry, rebellious or restless. However, perhaps we, as caregiver, feel that there is nonetheless some room to take an extra step. Perhaps space arises to talk, for example, about angels, spirit guides or moved on family members awaiting the soul.

To remain within the spiritual practice of the dying person is also of significant importance for people who lived a religious life. The idea is that to a Catholic dying person we communicate within the Catholic thoughts, for example, about Jesus, Maria and the angels. Using familiar practices sorts more effect than talking about reincarnation and mantras.

Flower remedies; essential oils; stone elixirs; Aura-Soma

There are many possibilities to assist the dying person in his process using remedies. These remedies affect the energy body of a human being and as such the human being in his entirety. The most effective are remedies carrying a very powerful positive message. They work at the astral body of a human being - exactly the body that plays a vital role for the dying person. Remedies are available related to all issues in life. In relation to the process of dying, we can think of the following themes:

- The fear of dying.

- The opening of the heart; forgiveness.

- Letting go.

- Tuning the mind to the light.

- Being open to support and help from the spiritual world.

Some examples

- *The flower remedy 'Oak' of the brand Bach aids in finding balance in persevering and letting go, so typical for letting go during the process of dying.*

- *The flower remedy 'Mustard' of the brand Bach helps to make the transformation from the dark to the light.*

- *The stone elixir 'Diamond' of the brand Alaskan Essences assists the soul in becoming aware of the inner divine Spark.*

- *The essential oil of Tulsi (Ocimum sanctum) helps the human being to open to the divine.*

- *The light violet quintessence 'Saint Germain' of the brand Aura-Soma helps the soul to be aware of his divine core. It is the most calming quintessence of Aura-Soma.*

The dying person is very receptive to this type of remedies. When a flower remedy bottle is placed next to the bed, it usually suffices. Oils can be evaporated. Aura-Soma remedies can be put on the skin or can be introduced into the aura by placing a few drops at the hands and then moving these hands through the aura of the dying person. The beauty of these remedies is that they also operate when the brain does not function well any longer, or if someone does not see or hear well. Think about the people in a coma who are capable of perceiving and remembering everything, while their brains and senses are completely non-functioning. The perception and the memorisation occur in the subtle astral body of the person, and that is exactly where these remedies work.

In this book, there is no opportunity to explain how these remedies are chosen. It is discussed in most detail in the book *Energetic Protection*. All the above-mentioned remedies are freely available. It means that they can be bought and used by everyone. They are very well suited to assist the dying person in his process of moving on. On the Internet, much information can be found about the workings of these remedies and how to use them. We recommend that palliative care organisation obtain more knowledge about this type of remedies. There is more in the world than the chemical drugs typically offered by Western medicine.

Praying, meditation, mantras

What is praying? What is meditating? Different people will reply differently to these questions. We give our opinions. When praying we focus ourselves at the higher realms. This higher realm is in the first place ourselves because it is where God lives as our divine Spark. Praying is foremost an inward movement where we focus at the highest and purest in ourselves, our divine core. This magnificent divine essence is present in everyone. Also in the soul that has moved on.

People have lived on earth that were fully in contact with their divine Spark; their person and divine core were one. Within Christianity, there are Jesus and Maria. Within Hinduism there is Krishna, and within Buddhism there is Buddha. These indescribable beautiful people are helping humankind. They are, always and everywhere, focused on their helping task. We may turn to them and ask them for assistance, and also pray. Whether we focus at the divine in ourselves or the divine as manifested in Jesus, Maria, Krishna or Buddha, real prayers are heard within the laws of the human development. Prayers expressed with great love and strength put in motion an enormous energy. They fill the room with light and power. They are an enormous support for the person moving on. A prayer can take the form of existing prayers, such as Ave Maria, but also of direct language from the heart.

The goal of meditation is to find calm and to relax and to connect deeply with ourselves and our Self from this peace and relaxation. Meditation can bring forth a beautiful energy in the room. It aids the dying as well as the helping person to transcend the pain body. It also provides more energy, which can be welcome during the long days that are often associated with the process of dying.

Mantras stem from the Eastern tradition. They are equally deeply rooted as the Our father in the Catholic tradition. Mantras have a profound meaning. Mantras can bring forth fields of light, peace and love in the direct environment of a dying person. They support the dying person in his tuning into the light.

An important mantra in the Hindu tradition is the Gayatri mantra. In the Gayatri mantra, light is being called to protect us and to help us in our development regarding contact with our divine Spark. In the Tibetan Buddhism, the most prominent mantra is the mantra of compassion: *aum mani padme hum*. When you are chanting this mantra, the blessing is requested of the Buddha Avalokiteshvara. This never ending being of compassion has promised to free all beings that are capable of feeling from the world of reincarnation. This mantra helps us to release our negative characteristics and strengthens our positive characteristics. This mantra has enormous powers. The more a dying person has used the blessing of the mantra in his daily life, the most powerful these blessings will enter him during the process of dying. It directly illustrates the possibilities and limitations of using mantras. In general, it is best to stay closest to the tradition of the dying person. To a Catholic familiar with the Catholic tradition, the Ave Maria and Our father are beautiful prayers. The Ave Maria can also be used as background music to fill the room with spiritual vibrations.

Praying, meditation, and singing or playing mantras or Ave Maria are powerful sources of healing and uplifting energy during the process of dying. If needed, they can be played continuously, such that the music is blessing day and night.

The atmosphere around the dying person

Eric is dying. He is a profound spiritual being who is certain he will continue to live. He has accepted his death. He is feeling the beings of Light around him, who are there to collect him. He is grateful for it. He has complete faith in the future. Then Henry, his ex-colleague, is coming to say goodbye. Before he entered, Henry was calling his wife, and they talked about the holidays, which made him happy. Now Henry is entering the room. Eric is DYING. Eric will be DEAD soon. This fact does not ask for happiness or power, is Henry's opinion. He puts on a sombre face. His face is communicating Suffering. Based on Pity, he is talking with Eric. The pleasant energy in the room disappears entirely. Moreover, it is replaced by a heaviness...

People who are dying are grateful for light, for kindness, and for sincere love. It forms an atmosphere that is feeding them during their process of moving on. We do not have to feel ashamed for light energy when we are visiting a dying person. Focus your attention on the higher aspect. Bring a refined, pure energy in the room for the quality of the spirit. Let us support the dying person rather than that he has to carry us!

Anna enters the room where a dear friend is dying. She connects with the calm in her. She transcends the emotions. Her heart radiates love, her being light. She makes eye contact with the dying person. Her eyes encourage him. Her eyes communicate that all will be fine. I love you, and I am here with you. Let go, it is fine. You are allowed to go. Anna sits down next to her friend. She is holding his hand and is going inward connecting even deeper with herself. She embraces the silence in her. Just by itself words of love come to her, which she silently communicates. She is grateful for this deep contact. When saying goodbye she promises her friend she will send him love the coming days, and the days afterward. After she has left, her friend falls asleep peacefully. It is good as it is. He can let go. He relaxes and releases. It is over and is allowed to be over. He approaches the Light. He knows it. Anna's eyes show what he is feeling inside...

In this example, Anna shows how beautiful it is when the helper is in deep contact with him or herself. It is a blessing for the dying person.

At times, the pain of the approaching death is so intense, that it blows us away. Inside we are one big wound. For example, when a child had a car accident and will be dying within the next few days. Alternatively, when we are 32, having three children and our husband is having an unexpected heart attack and is to live only a very short while. Although our big heart would be our best help, it might in such circumstances not be possible to connect with it. We feel beaten, destroyed. However, there are probably moments that things are better. Those moments can be used to connect at a deeper level with ourselves and the person moving on. Use those moments to talk, and to remember together the good and beautiful moments. Use them to explain what is happening when someone is dying: for example how the angels will come to help the soul.

Help from the astral world

The weeks before the actual death are a busy time for the dying person. We are not talking about the doctors and the nurses. Neither about the people helping. We are talking about the beings from the astral world that prepare the dying person for his journey to the new world. Who are those beings? In the first place family members. It can be deceased family members from this life, but also previous lives. Souls that share a deep blood relation, in this or earlier lives, often help the dying person to move on. During the process of dying the soul detaches bit by bit from the body. The soul is active in the astral world. It is extensively lectured about what is to be expected. Also guiding spirits take part in this coaching. Some people take on this guiding job in their sleep, when they leave their body. Their soul is still connected to their body ethereally. Sometimes therapeutic work is done in addition. The dying person is being assisted in opening the cage around his heart, such that love is getting a chance - love that determines the quality of the future life in the astral world.

On wings of Light...

Not only souls of human beings are visiting. Also, angels are intensely involved in helping the dying person. Angels are no fairy tale; they are actual beings. Their tasks include helping human beings at birth and death. Angels are in the first place beings of Light. It encompasses that they are ultimately serving toward the creation. As a result, they live in wholeness, close to God. This wholeness they experience as love. Moreover, all those hundred thousands of people who have told they have had contact with an angel, always speak about that never ending big love and that magnificent light. Because angels are so light, they know very well what leads to the light and what makes a human being stray. At their level of development, compromises on their path to the light are no longer possible. They are unconditionally loving in their supporting of the human being. However, at the same time they are entirely clear in their observation of the road that the human being is taking: this behaviour brings you closer to your inner Source; that behaviour leads away from it! Angels are thus also just and strict. The latter is a good thing, because it helps us to open the eyes to the truth of the road toward our inner Self.

Angels always come and help when the human being is moving on. Some people surrender gratefully to their guidance and advice. Others do not want anything to do with their help. The choice a person makes is related to his human psyche. It might be that someone regards himself as too bad a person to be worthy of being approached by angels. Alternatively, someone cannot imagine that such a love exists... and thus cannot perceive it! It is how the psycho-plastic world operates. This concept seems farfetched, but even in our world, strong examples of it exist. For example, it is recorded that the Indians did not see the ships of the Western people when they first came - because they had never seen ships, and thus they could not exist to them. Those big ships arrived, but they could not see them! Similarly, it is hard for some people to perceive the world of angels.

When people die, they often go through a process of suffering. Nonetheless, at times, we are seeing calmness arise in the last days, and a peaceful smile decorates the face. The smile is caused by the contact with the angels and helpers from the astral world. The soul feels so uplifted by what she has seen that all the suffering is no longer relevant. She knows what can be expected, and this gives rise to a beautiful serene smile.

At the last exhalation, the heart stops beating. There is no longer a pupil reflex. Clinically, a person is dead. It means that the body no longer functions. However, the physical body is only one part of the human being. The astral body and the divine Spark now detach from the physical body. The astral body is now in charge of feeling, knowing, thinking, seeing and hearing.

What would be pleasant for the soul at this moment? What is the most beautiful we can wish for the soul at this moment? In our opinion, these are respect, deep love, silence, simplicity and above all: prayer. It is the moment to call the Beings of Light that the deceased person loved during his life: the angels, Jesus, Maria, Buddha, enlightened masters, Krishna or whichever saint.

The moment of death is a key moment, at which the soul can make a tremendous leap. When Mahatma Gandhi was shot dead, he immediately spoke the mantra *Rama, Rama, Rama* ... Rama is one of the names of God in the East. By placing the attention at the moment of detaching of the soul uniformly at God, the soul goes straight to God. In the English version of the movie, Mahatma Gandhi does not speak Rama, Rama, Rama, but 'Oh my God, Oh my God'. Gandhi was focused on God all of his life. He had been trained to immediate turn to God at the moment of death. Not in the sense, 'Oh my God, what is happening to me now', because this sentence is part of the emotional domain. Gandhi directly turned to God, in complete spiritual conscience. Here, we see again how dying represents life. At the moment of death, the body relies on routines. Whoever has turned to God his whole life, will turn to God quickly at the moment of dying!

The last exhalation may contain powerful emotional energy. It is not desirable to inhale it as our principal teacher in Ayurveda has told us. Therefore, it is better to not bend over the face of a dying person in his last moments.

The last exhalation is a particularly spiritual moment, which does not combine well with medical procedures as we see it. The body has been given up. The soul is being born in the astral world. It is perfectly fine to make this a priority. It has a positive impact to take time for this phase. Determination of the death by a doctor can be done at a later stage, we think. This moment is for you, as a helper, to completely open your heart to God, to the Light, to the Beings of Light. It is the moment to encourage the person that has moved on to leap into the Light. There is a special technique that can be used for this purpose. It is described below.

Placing the dying or moved on person *in the light*

Placing someone in the light is a technique that is very dear to us, which explains why we describe it extensively. The human being comprises the physical body, the astral body and the divine Spark. The person is the entirety of his physical and astral body, which can only live thanks to his divine Spark. The person is aware of this divine Spark only to some extent. The more a person is one with his divine Spark, the more loving a person is. Such people are magnificent people for their environment. Happiness arises by uniting with the divine Spark, regardless at which level. It is what we wish for every human being. However, how can a person learn that he is not all those confusing and at times annoying and painful emotions? How can it be transferred that a beautiful sun is shining inside, despite all the evident suffering? It is possible using the method that we call *placing someone in the light.*

Imagine we like to place Aimy in the light. We focus inward. Within ourselves (ideally in our big heart) we see an image of Aimy. We then see that from Aimy's heart pure bright white light is radiating. It is not the light of the helper (you) that the helper (you) uses to fill Aimy. It is light coming from the divine Spark in Aimy herself. This magnificent clear white light is radiating from the heart of Aimy and filling her whole body. It is also radiating through her skin outward filling her aura. We perform this activity with great inner clarity, purity, and determination. We know: the divine Spark is filling Aimy entirely and radiating through her outward. We retain this image preferably several minutes, in all calm.

The reason this technique works is the following: each thought, each imagination, each emotion forms an energy field at the subtle, for the human being invisible, level. The energy flows where the attention is directed. When we focus on Aimy, all our thoughts, images and feelings flow as energetic messages toward Aimy. Aimy's energetic body receives these messages clearly. The message of the image that we are working with is: you are your divine Self. This message is as a fresh breeze on a summer day, or as the sun showing herself on a cold day. She is reminding the conscience of Aimy of the Love in herself, of her Heart. She becomes aware that there is a magnificent Source of Love present in her heart.

Thoughts are travelling extremely fast as energy. So fast that distance is irrelevant. Regardless of the distance between Aimy and us, we will always reach her within a fraction of a second. We can thus place Aimy in the light while we are sitting next to her. We can also do it when we are travelling home. We can do it when we are hundreds or thousands of kilometres apart. The effect is the same, as the distance is irrelevant.

What is important is how we offer this image to Aimy, our intention behind it. Everybody is free to choose his path. Everyone is blessed with free will. The principle of free will underlies the creation. You see it back in how we like to offer the image to Aimy. We communicate: 'we see you in this manner: as a being of light.' Nothing else. It is up to Aimy to absorb this image within herself, to investigate it, to embrace it or if she chooses so to reject it. The power should be aimed at our own inner resolve: 'This is you; this is how I see you.' When the attention is aimed at us wanting the other to accept it, it gets a coercing character. It will lead to rejection rather than to acceptance.

When we place Aimy in the light, we only aim at the absolute inner knowledge that Aimy is light. It is what we know and nothing else. It is how it functions most powerfully. We are not investigating intuitively how deeply the soul Aimy absorbs this message. Would we do so, we would no longer be focused on the inner knowing that Aimy is light, but put it up for discussion: gone is the power of our inner image!

Placing in the light can be done through an inner image as explained earlier. It can also be performed through words. Words to place someone in the light are: *You are your inner divine Self.* Naturally other words bringing the same message can also be used. A different option to put someone in the light is through feeling. Some people are mostly feeling in nature. It is their most powerful option. Feel that Aimy radiates magnificent love. Become totally happy and joyful of the magnificent love she radiates. Placing in the light can thus be achieved through images, thoughts and feelings. Each combination is possible as well. The most powerful is using what we are good at!

When someone is dying, for example, a parent of a partner, also painful and negative memories can surface, for example, abuse. When a parent is abusing his child, the relationship of this person and his divine Spark is frail. The voice of God does not reach his acts. Would the connection have been proper, the abuse would not have taken place. When a parent in the above example dies, it is of great importance that the child transcends this personal suffering. He can do so by placing the parent in the light. Doing so, he shows him or her the unity of body, soul and spirit. He helps the parent to move on to the world of light.

8 The first days after death

A person has moved on, and much is asked of those being left behind. So much that has to be arranged. So many emotions maybe as well. What is important in these days? Although the physical body is dead, the soul still is in the birth channel to the other world. Often, the soul will stay close to the body for some time. It is hearing and seeing everything that the people around his body are communicating. He is feeling their intentions. It illustrates how close the soul is at that moment. How would we want ourselves to be treated when we have just died, knowing that we perceive everything what is happening around our body? Most probably, we want to be treated with respect and love. How would it feel to us if we would be present as soul, very much alive, and all people around us would talk about us as if we are not there? As if we are dead, and no longer among the living, but just being a dead body. Maybe we would want to scream: 'I am not dead. I am alive. I see you, hear you, feel you.'

What could help the soul that is moving on? Because the soul can hear us, feel us and read our intentions accurately, we are continuously connected with this soul, even if we do not know it ourselves. The first days are critical days to the soul. These days are her chance. When the soul connects with the light during these days, she will be born into a world of light in the astral world. We can help the soul in connecting with the light by ourselves being an environment of light and creating one. The idea is rather simple.

Creating an atmosphere of light supports the process of dying and it continues to do so in the days after death. It can be very helpful when the physical space in which the body is present is also pleasant. Allowing an atmosphere in which we can be quiet, and can be ourselves; where we can meditate and pray. Where we can express words to the soul that are private and thus require a protective environment. Ideally the body is laid out in his home, close to people he loves and who love him. The room can be beautifully decorated, such that the space has a harmonising effect on visitors. It is nice if there are flowers. Burning candles raise the energy level. Music can contribute to the quality of the atmosphere, also for the soul moving on. The people close to the body or those visiting will be affected by it and taken to the dimension of the music. Therefore, it is important that the music be spiritual, that it bears witness of true love and life after death. This music can also call for help, such as in Ave Maria and the higher mantras. Also in this phase, it is pleasant and helpful when music is being played that the deceased person can relate to.

To keep the room fresh

In the room, where a person dies, and potentially also will be laid out, much intense information (energy) is present. It is probably in the first place energy of the deceased person himself. Also in the days after death emotional energy of the deceased person is released into the space where the body is present. Moreover, logically also energy of people that came to visit is present. This energy can linger in the room. People visiting at a later stage are picking up this energy quicker and would then also connect with their pain body. To the soul this means that the space, in which she is staying, is filled with sombre and dark colours. It is depressing and not aiding in taking her next step on her journey to the light.

How can we create a clean atmosphere, such that the emotional energy is discharged or transformed in an appropriate manner? There are endless possibilities to do so. We name a few.

- Letting fresh air in regularly by opening windows is an obvious option. It is also very practical and readily applicable. It is always helpful. The wind will take the emotional energy. So open the windows while the curtains are also open. In this manner, we optimally benefit from the wind. Wind is one of the reasons why people find it helpful to walk outside. The wind cleanses them. The emotional charge disappears to some extent. Again and again, air the room, each time we feel the room is airless.

- Burning candles bring light into a room. Candlelight cleanses the space. There can be a sea of light - tea lights are also excellent - day and night.

- Incense has been used for thousands of years - everywhere in the world! - because of its cleansing effect. Not all incense is cleansing. Cheap incense often contains chemical substances that pollute the air instead of cleanse. Good, cleansing incense is often more expensive, because the cleansing ingredient, sandalwood, is precious. Use incense that states sandalwood has been used to produce it. When such incense is cheap, you know it cannot be correct! Incense can also contain sandalwood powder or the essential oil of sandalwood. The latter can be worked into the powder, but also the bamboo core of incense can be drenched in the essence. The latter is the best sandalwood incense. It is advisable to burn incense a few times a day.

- Flowers have a pleasant impact on the environment in which they are placed. White and pink flowers are the flowers well suited to open the heart to love and purity. It also aids the soul that has moved on to transform her energy to higher areas of truth and purity. This aspect cannot be underestimated.

- Praying is a fantastic way to cleanse the space - given we touch a high and pure part in ourselves when praying. When we pray from despair, lack of power and victimisation, the environment will be polluted with negative emotional energy. When we pray in a positive manner, we bring much light into the space. The room can benefit from it tremendously. When someone has prayed like this, the place definitely feels different afterward. The area feels light, blessed, and pleasant to be.

- White light has the potential to get stagnated energy moving and transform it to a higher conscience. The power of it is limitless. In this situation, we usually use light as visualisation by visualising white light in the room.

- The room can also be cleansed using flower remedies, essential oils and sprays of the brand Aura-Soma. Choosing these remedies can be done intuitively or selected clinically based on symptoms and knowledge of the areas in which the remedy works. These remedies can also be tested using (auto)-kinesiologically techniques or using a pendulum. Both require a level of expertise to guarantee reliable and valid results. Concerning the theme of this book, we describe several remedies that in general can be helpful in these circumstances. When possible, proper testing or choosing intuitively is preferred. The flower remedy and the essential oil can be evaporated in the room using an evaporating device for essential oil. Some drops of the chosen flower remedy can also be added to water in a clean plant spray. After you shake the mixture, it can be sprayed into the air.

- The below remedies can be ordered through the Internet.

  - *A very useful flower remedy is 'Mycena' of Bloesem Remedies Nederland.*

  - *We recommend the essential oils of the (white) rose and sandalwood. Select a trustworthy producer of essential oils.*

  - *Aura-Soma is a producer of remedies based on a particular combination of colour, essential oils, flower remedies and mineral elixirs. It is a proven system. To cleanse a space we recommend the spray Pomander dark magenta. To refine the energy in the room, in other words, to bring it to a higher vibration, we advise the spray Serapis Bey.*

Praying

Through praying, we can transfer a tremendous amount of light to the soul. It is a unique method of being attentive. It is a very concentrated space. Praying can take place in a wide variety of ways. Below we share some of our ideas regarding praying. To find your path - also within this framework - is very meaningful. Praying is positive energy. The prayer is directed at the light. It may originate in despair and suffering, but the prayer is to be light in itself. Let us explain.

In a prayer, the human being directs himself to the higher. He is asking the higher for help on his path, or for other people or souls. He is calling for help from souls or powers that are more evolved regarding their path to God than he is himself. He can also direct his prayers directly to God, as his inner Self, or as God, who is carrying the entire creation. It requires faith that those forces are present. It needs hope: hope that these forces help. It also asks for courage to delegate and (partly) let go of having control. When we know very deeply inside that there are forces that help us, our prayers gain so much power, so much positive energy. We are setting in motion what we are radiating. When we radiate belief, inner knowing, hope and faith, we free large forces in the world. These forces relate to our questions asked out of love for the deceased.

To whom can we address our prayer for the deceased person? Maria, mother of Jesus, is the divine Mother. We can always directly ask for her help. She is there where people are asking assistance. Always and everywhere. We do not have to doubt. To many deceased people Jesus is familiar, close and thus also accessible. Then there are naturally also angels. Angels are important helpers for humankind. They support the human being in many different ways. They are present to help everyone's birth as well as during the process of dying. While helping they honour free will. There are also endless testimonies of people that have experienced how an angel saved them from death. It illustrates how powerful the presence of angels is in our dimension. Many people also experience the vibration, the energy of the angels. Let us open our heart to the angels. Let us dare ask them for help!

Jesus, Maria and the angels are the primary helpers within the Christian traditions. Maria and Jesus are the pillars of the Western spiritual tradition and as such very accessible to us. They have been with us for generations. They are familiar. We can also address saints in this tradition. A few decades ago, Western people were still very familiar with saints. At this moment, the saints of the Christian tradition are far less widely known.

Also outside the Christian tradition there are beautiful helpers. The best known in the Western world are possibly Buddha's. Buddha's are enlightened masters. Some of them have taken up the task to help humankind. They form a collective field of enormous force in the cosmos. We can also pray to them to help the deceased person after his death. Very special are the Buddha's of the Tibetan Buddhism, because Tibetan Buddhism is specialised in the dying person and the soul that has just moved on. Through the mantra *Aum mani padme aum* a field of light is called forth.

In general, we can best address those powers that are familiar to the deceased person. The deceased soul is then more open, such that the power being called upon can be better received. Praying always operates within the boundaries of free will. When someone chooses to go a different path, for example not opening to light, love and truth, it is being respected. It is a divine law underlying the human development. Wherever free will is not respected, there is dark energy.

How do we address the helping major Sources of Light? When we open our heart and are grateful for these powers, they are instantly with us. Gratitude is the primary motivator. Gratitude is a dimension of the heart. We are grateful that this power is available, that we may call forth this power for help and that it is putting effort in the development of the individual human being. Gratitude opens something very deep in the human being and the cosmos. It sets such refined forces in motion. Gratitude also comprises we have faith that this power is there for us. Gratitude excludes doubt. It is paramount at the level of us being helpers

Placing in the light

In chapter seven, we described the technique placing in the light. It is valuable to apply this method also in the first days after death. The aim of the technique is to help the deceased soul in being aware of his divine core.

To stay three days and nights close to the deceased body

In many cultures, it is recommended to be with the deceased person day and night and pray for him. Day and night. Three days long... Have you ever done this? Most people have not. Still it might be a wonderful opportunity for everybody. It releases something beautiful and refined in us. It is a chance of which only few are offered in life. Three days of praying means we go inward intensely, to the space in ourselves in which there are light and hope. To love and truth. To contact with other worlds that have to tell us so much about our lives and ourselves. Three days of intense deepening.

What a chance as well for the deceased person. Three long days of receiving positive energy. Three days of being tuned into the highest and the most precious there is. Three days of being lifted above all confusion of the moment. It is wonderful, almost too good to be true.

We can give this to someone that has passed away. It is nice to do it together with a few others. To agree who is at which times with the body and praying, everyone in his way. Many practical issues have to be tackled in the first days after death. People also need to sleep and eat. There are children that need attention, and visitors. There is so much to do. However, let's not forget what is most important in this phase: helping the soul to reach the Light. We can be of immensely beautiful help in this. When we want to organise it, a lot is possible, especially in these days. We can free time that is usually filled with work or daily tasks. In this period, we can put aside many obligations. Everyone understands this and will not make a fuss about it. It is a chance.

When we pray for three days, we get to another space with ourselves. However, also with the deceased person. Maybe the person is our parent, sister, brother, uncle, aunt or even our child. In these days, we can get to such a fine attunement that a lot of unresolved issues dissolve. Stagnant pain dissolves. In those days, we experience a lot. Perhaps also, the pain regarding the loss of other people is surfacing. These days help us to handle this in a profound manner, by being close to ourselves and to pray, day after day. When the person we are praying for is very dear to us, and when dying is seen as premature, the pain can be very profound. We acknowledge this. We also understand that the process of digesting the pain can be long and complicated. Still these three days can also mean a lot to us because deep within we have different contact with ourselves.

When three days have been spent praying around the body of the deceased, a powerful field of higher energy arises. It fills the space in which we are. All people visiting to say goodbye, feel it. The farewell is then experienced differently. For the deceased person, It translates to increasing amounts of light coming toward him. Let us just imagine that we as a soul are present with our deceased body and dark, heavy, and sombre energy is continuously approaching it from the people that are saying goodbye to us. It would not make us happy! It does not uplift us. That is why it is important to fill the space with light, light and even more light.

When the body is in a mortuary

When a person dies in a hospital, his body is often quickly brought to the mortuary. With its temperature-controlled environment the mortuary stops the process of decay. From hygienic perspective, it is an effective strategy. However, the soul of the deceased person does not remain in a pleasant, uplifting environment. The latter is not the point of focus of the hospital. In the mortuary, there is much despair, darkness and fear. It is not an environment where the soul is being aided in travelling to the light. That is why it is important to take action in order to help.

How can we do this? When the body can be brought home, a pleasant atmosphere can be created, which is indeed preferred. When it is not possible, there is an alternative: pretend the body is laid out at your house. You can decorate the space with the picture of the deceased person. It can be further supplied with flowers, beautiful candles, incense, music, mantras and anything else feeling good. Here we can pray as if the body is present because the distance does not matter. When our focus is aimed at the soul, the soul is with us, and we have contact. In addition to the soul coming to us attracted by the power of our love, our attention reaches the mortuary. The latter is helpful when the soul chooses to remain in the mortuary, for example, if she is not yet ready to release the body. Nothing can stop our soul to be in direct contact with the soul of the deceased person. Similar to when the body is physically present, we can pray three days and nights in our house in the area that we have chosen for it.

9 When the deceased soul is visiting us

Peter (36): I was in my bedroom. Suddenly I felt my father. He was very much present. To me, it was very clear he was indeed present.

Eva (6): Mummy told me that grandpa has died. Yesterday he was with me. He was standing in my room. I could see him. He was floating above my bed.

Eveline (46): When my mum died last year, I was in my house. I felt she was with me. I have seen her in my room that night.

Countless people experience that a deceased soul is visiting them. Within the context of this book, the deceased soul is family or a best friend who recently passed away and decided to visit. There is a need to say goodbye.

Alternatively, to inform that they are doing okay. It is the power of love that lifts the veil between both worlds. Some people are happy with this experience. Through it, they experience themselves that death does not exist. Some people are scared by it. Their fear is related to the unfamiliarity in society about souls without a body. However, why are we afraid? 'Tomorrow', we are the ones without a body. Then we live in the astral world. It is not all that special.

What can we do when a deceased soul is visiting us?

What would we wish to do when a deceased soul is coming to visit us? Is there still something to communicate? Now you are provided an opportunity! We can also ask questions. Maybe the deceased soul is in the capacity to contact us such that we can perceive what they want to tell us. On the other hand, we can rest assured that the soul will perceive us. She is listening and understanding not only our words, but also our feelings and thoughts. The soul is capable of communicating with us in many ways. The soul might choose to use a symbol language, because it is not possible for everyone to hear (clear hearing) or understand (clear knowing) her. Maybe her face or body is expressing what she wants to transfer.

Perhaps there is room for positive, loving contact. We open ourselves, and we remember a pleasant and precious moment that we experienced together. We wish the other the best in his new life. We give her courage and faith. We can also place the soul in the light as described earlier. We then point the soul to the path toward her divine Self. To the soul it is a valuable and powerful way to be in contact with us. We transcend the emotional confusion. We come closer in a way that makes both of us stronger.

When a soul keeps on coming

Sometimes deceased souls come to 'visit' for years. At times, they live with the family. Often this applies to a child in the family. In this case, there often is stagnation in the development of the soul. We go into more detail regarding this aspect later in the book.

10 The funeral or cremation

In this chapter, we discuss how we can help during the funeral or cremation. We do not consider the option funeral versus cremation. The ideas we present are applicable to both. The word funeral is used in the remainder of the text, but it can equally well be read as cremation.

A person has died. Carla was 36 when she died of cancer. Her children and husband have experienced the process in the last days as very intense. Carla is being buried. Who are present? In the first place, her mum who gave life to her. Her father, her siblings. Her husband and children. His family. Many friends and acquaintances. They all come to say goodbye and many, above all, to support the family by being present.

The soul of Carla is probably also present, attracted by the intensity of the thoughts and feelings directed at her. For sure there will be angels, beings of light who accompany her during this very intense day. Possibly there are also other souls from the astral world with Carla. How Carla will experience the day, is depending on Carla's soul herself, but also on the people attending the funeral. It is the focus of this chapter.

The emotion of a human being is an energy field at the astral level, which possesses a particular colour. There are emotions with dark, sombre colours. Emotions can look like grey areas of fog. Deep feelings of love are beautifully pink. The soul that is present at her funeral thus perceives the feelings of those present as areas of coloured energy. She is also feeling these fields.

At the funeral, there is logically also much deep pain and sorrow. There are worries and fear, and memories of the loss of other people we loved. All those emotions form sombre fields. When the coffin is carried to the grave, a cloud of grey energy at times surrounds the line of people. This energy is not pleasant to the soul. It is also a little bizarre. The soul is looking at her own funeral. Many people believe the person is no longer there while the soul perceives everything. To the soul it is very pleasant when there is light at his funeral. A light that arises due to love, due to faith in God, by calling for the angels, by prayers directed at the light in a positive manner.

There are so many beautiful things a person can do during a funeral benefiting the deceased person. Not every person present is capable of it. Firstly, most people that are present lack the knowledge. Moreover, for some the pain might be too big. However, people who have that knowledge and who are slightly more detached from the pain during the funeral can contribute much light. They can positively impact the dark mist so typical for some funerals. They can offer the deceased soul an anchor of light. To the soul it is comforting and very pleasant to be carried by those present in this light way. What can we do?

- We can connect with the most powerful and most beautiful part in us: our divine Spark. This divine Spark radiates magnificent clear white light from our heart chakra at the middle of our breastbone. We are light, bright clean white light. It has an enormous impact on the whole. It makes everything lighter, more bearable for others, but certainly for the soul that moved on.

- We can connect with the deceased soul. We can direct our attention to the soul and talk with her. We can send her our love, also if we have not known this person.

- We can call the angels. Do this in complete faith that they are supportive, and call based on hope rather than despair. Ask the angels to bless and guide the soul that has just moved on. Ask the soul to surrender to it, such that she can perceive and experience the angels. Perhaps the soul has turned away at this moment of the possibility that something like angels exists. Our help can make a difference: through our love it might be possible to open the eyes and heart of the deceased soul to these exceptional beings. What a blessing for the deceased soul when that may happen.

- Maybe it is possible during the service for the people present to, together, thank the soul for the good she has done. It can be in any shape and form. Below, we give a suggestion. The setting can be a church, but also the room in which the cremation ceremony is taking place.

I want to ask you to direct your thoughts toward Carla. Carla is dead. However, to me her soul continues to live. I am also confident that she is here with us today. Her soul is seeing and hearing us, perceiving our feelings. Would it not be beautiful if we, together, give Carla strength? If we help her to release this world with a good feeling. We can do this now. Therefore, I invite you to do so, in all freedom. I encourage you to remember the good in Carla. Something that made you both laugh, something that made you both happy. Something you were proud of in her. Something she did well. Something small, something big, the result is the same: we send positive energy to Carla. Imagine, positive energy from all these people. That feels wonderful for Carla. It brings much love to Carla. Bring back those beautiful moments. Remember the moment, in which she did a good thing... Carla, we thank you for all the good you have done for us. We wish you a magnificent and blessed journey. We wish you are very close to God.

11 Help when death has been unexpected and traumatic

Some people die wholly unexpected. For example in a car accident or through acute heart failure. At times also through violence. Death can be there all of a sudden whether we are twenty or eighty. What happens when death takes us by surprise? How is the soul of the deceased person dealing with it? There has not been any time to prepare for the person himself or the family. Neither could angels, nor guides initiate death during the deathbed.

To the soul, a sudden death is very traumatic, as it is for the people around them. Often the soul cannot initially comprehend what has happened. Do not forget that the astral world, in which the soul is living, forms after her feelings and thoughts. Thus, it can happen that someone who is fatally hit by a car continues to go to his house. He is present at his home and continues with his routines, initially as if nothing has happened. Gradually, the soul becomes aware that something is amiss. However, what? Some souls open themselves to the possibility that they are dead. They have knowledge about dying and life after death. This knowledge is their saving. Because through this knowledge they can direct themselves to the world of light and continue travelling to the light. Angels are also capable of giving them guidance while the soul is on this path. The souls are being awaited for and gradually coached toward the world they will live in from now on. Step by step. However, the first step is awareness that the body is dead, the soul alive and one can travel toward the light.

To help these souls is crucial and beautiful. It often is not complicated or hard. People who were closest to the deceased person have the best chance to connect with the soul. Love is the bridge. Kind, tender words lead the soul inward where love for herself is present. They connect her with her heart, where light is, and love and hope. Then tell the soul what has happened. Explain that she has died and what were the circumstances of her death. Tell her that she is ALIVE, because she has contact with us while she is actually dead. Explain her that she is now living in the astral world and that it is imperative to focus on the light. We would explain using the following words.

The world, in which you are now, forms after what you are feeling and thinking. Therefore direct all your attention to the good and the beautiful. Focus on God, on love, on peace, on the pure. Do it NOW. See what happens? The world around you changes. It is the key to your future. Continue to focus on the light, and then you will proceed further, in continuous lighter, more loving environments. In your world, there are angels to help you. Open your heart to them, and then you can talk with them, and see them. Open your heart to them and call them. Do it NOW... See there they are. We ask the angels that are with you to help you on your path to the light. We wish you a blessed journey.

Ask the angels to guide this soul. Then let go and leave it in the hands of God.

12 The first months after death

In the first months after death, each soul is further developing. The most important question is whether the soul has arrived well in the other world. We mean whether the soul has started to live in the astral world together with souls without a body or whether the soul has been hovering in the world of people. We already explained that the latter could happen for a variety of reasons. It is naturally up to the soul to go her way and choose to do so. However, we may indeed offer help on that path. It will make a significant difference to place the soul in the light. Because in doing so we help the soul to remember that she is more than the emotions and confusion, she is likely experiencing. In addition, the soul is connected with the Light in herself, resulting in her environment becoming light. When we keep on repeating this, we remind the soul again and again of her inner Source. Again and again, in all calm, in all faith, in all freedom. It is a way in which we, being on earth, can help the soul in her journey to the Light.

The first months are important to both ourselves, being left behind, and to the deceased soul. When we are placing the soul continuously in the light, we not only do something exquisite for the deceased soul. We also help ourselves. We transcend the pain. We are not powerless, but can help. There is contact! We know that we are precious to the soul. It gives us strength and courage to keep going.

Logically we do not have to do this all by ourselves. There are magnificent beings of light that love to hear our prayer. Praying works! Also in the months after death it is very meaningful to pray for the soul of the deceased person. We may address God, Jesus, Maria, the angels, the enlightened Masters, Buddha's, and/or others we feel spiritually connected to. Time and again, we are allowed to ask for help for the deceased soul on her path. It works most beautiful when we do this from a positive mind-set, from the joy that we may do so and can ask, knowing that our prayers are heard.

Positive energy it thus essential for the soul of the deceased person. Also, when we are together as a family it is beautiful to send energy to the deceased soul. We can do this, for example, by talking about the good qualities and deeds of the deceased person. Whatever we express at such a moment, reaches the soul of the deceased person!

We are connected to our ancestors as pearls in a string. Long after their physical death, souls that have lived together continue to impact each other. That is also why it is important to help the soul on her path to the light.

13 To help when the soul does not let go of our world

In chapter nine, we have seen that souls sometimes seek contact with their loved ones in the first days after death. In chapter eleven, attention has been given to souls whose bodies died traumatically. These souls could remain in the world of the people and seek contact in an improper manner. There are also other reasons why souls are not continuing their path to the light well after the death of their body.

One reason is attachment to people here. Sometimes a soul wants also to care for people here, for example, small children, a sick partner or parent. At times, the soul has a strong attachment to the place where she has always lived and into which she has put much effort. She does not want to give up this place. There can also be fear for what lies ahead. It could, for example, arise because someone has made big mistakes in his life and is afraid for the consequences in the hereafter.

Thus, there are many souls who do not move on directly after their death. They continue to 'hangout' in the world of people. It explains the countless experiences of people with deceased souls. It is important that these souls be helped. When the soul contacting you is familiar, it can be advisable to start a conversation. Explain that she is not meant to be here but that she is supposed to grow to the light.

Some souls contacting you do not feel pleasant. It asks for expertise to interact with this kind of souls and show them their path. Therefore, it is for many people certainly better to have no contact with them. What you can do, is asking Jesus, Maria, angels, or another source one relates to, to help such a soul. It might also be advisable to seek help from experts in this field.

14 Conclusions

Life and death are tightly connected. We cannot ignore it. It is important that we prepare for death by acquiring knowledge about death and what life looks like after death. Knowledge is abundantly present. It is of tremendous value to help the dying persons and their souls in their moving on.

Suggestions for further reading

Delnooz, F., Martinot, P., *Energetic protection*

Delnooz, F., Martinot, P., *Dealing with emotions, effectively, easily*, www.de-verbinding.com/books

Rinpoche, S., *The Tibetan book of living and dying*

Thurman, R.A.F., *The Tibetan book of the dead*

About the authors

As senior coaches/therapists, Fons Delnooz and Patricia Martinot have been studying and working in the field of helping people for more than 30 years. They work with people of all ages and backgrounds on an individual basis, as well as with groups, and offer training and coaching for professionals (mostly therapists and coaches). They deal with a wide variety of issues in personal development and are specialized in working with Highly Sensitive People (HSP). Based on the work they have done with clients, they have written and published ten books in Dutch, some of which have been translated into German, Spanish and English.

They can be best contacted through their website: www.de-verbinding.com.